DEADLY DISASTERS

Massacre at Virginia Tech

Disaster & Survival

Richard Worth

Enslow Publishers, Inc.
40 Industrial Road
Box 398
Berkeley Heights, NJ 07922
USA

http://www.enslow.com

Library of Congress Cataloging-in-Publication Data

Worth, Richard.
    Massacre at Virginia Tech : disaster & survival / Richard Worth.
        p. cm. — (Deadly disasters)
    Summary: "Examines the tragic school shooting at Virginia Tech University, detailing the horrifying massacre, the lives of the killer and victims, and the sociological problems surrounding school shootings"—Provided by publisher.
    Includes bibliographical references and index.
    ISBN-13: 978-0-7660-3274-3
    ISBN-10: 0-7660-3274-4
    1. Virginia Tech Massacre, Blacksburg, Va., 2007. 2. Cho, Seung-Hui, 1984–2007. 3. Mass murder—Virginia—Blacksburg. 4. School shootings—Virginia—Blacksburg. 5. Campus violence—Virginia—Blacksburg.
    6. Virginia Polytechnic Institute and State University—Students. I. Title.
    HV6534.B53W67 2008
    364.152'309755785—dc22
                          2007025592

Printed in the United States of America

10 9 8 7 6 5 4 3 2 1

Illustration Credits: Associated Press, pp. 1, 4, 8, 9, 10, 12, 17, 18, 20, 21, 24, 26, 28, 29, 31, 32, 35, 36, 38, 40; Enslow Publishers, Inc., p. 6.

Cover Illustration: Associated Press.

Contents

1 Murder on Campus 5

2 The Victims 11

3 Portrait of a Killer 19

4 Why Did He Commit
Mass Murder? 25

5 Gun Control 30

6 After the Disaster 34

Deadliest School Shootings in
the United States 42

Chapter Notes 43

Glossary 46

Further Reading and Internet Addresses 47

Index 48

This graphic shows the Virginia Tech campus and retraces the events on April 16, 2007, when a gunman went on a shooting rampage. The massacre started at a dormitory called West Ambler Johnston Hall.

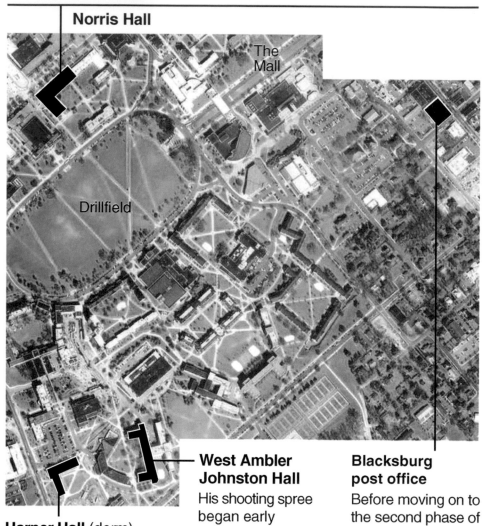

Norris Hall

The Mall

Drillfield

West Ambler Johnston Hall

His shooting spree began early Monday at the West Ambler Johnston Hall dorm where he killed one male and one female.

Blacksburg post office

Before moving on to the second phase of his attack at Norris Hall, Cho took time to mail a package containing video to NBC News.

Harper Hall (dorm)

Gunman Seung-Hui Cho lived in the Harper Hall on the South end of campus.

SOURCES: Virginia Tech; witness accounts, GeoEye   AP

Murder on Campus

BLACKSBURG, VIRGINIA, APRIL 16, 2007, SHORTLY *after 7:00 A.M.* The early morning quiet of Virginia Polytechnic Institute, also known as Virginia Tech, was shattered suddenly by gunfire. The shot rang out from the fourth floor of West Ambler Johnston Hall dormitory.

Freshman Emily Hilscher, who had planned to become a veterinarian, had been shot in her dorm room. At the sound of gunfire, resident advisor Ryan Clark came out of his room. He too was gunned down and killed. The killer exited the dorm, leaving bloody footprints.

West Ambler Johnston Hall, 7:30 A.M. By this time, local police detectives had arrived. They questioned Heather Haugh, a friend of Hilscher's. The discussions focused on Hilscher's boyfriend, Karl Thornhill. "They assumed it was something domestic, that he was after her," Haugh said.[1] Police suspected Thornhill had killed Hilscher in an angry fight. They guessed Clark had been

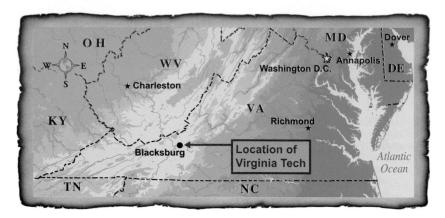

Virginia Tech is located in Blacksburg, Virginia, which is west of the capital of Richmond. killed because he was in the wrong place at the wrong time. The police learned that Thornhill owned guns.

Haugh said, Thornhill and Hilscher had an "amazing relationship." She also told police that he "wasn't violent."[2] The police searched his house for the gun that killed Hilscher and Clark. They did not find it because Thornhill was not the killer.

Burress Hall, 8:25 A.M. In an emergency meeting, Virginia Tech president Charles Steger and his advisors were trying to decide what to do to protect other students. Steger was undecided. What if he ordered students out of their classrooms and the lone gunman reappeared? By 9:30 A.M., reports came into the president's office of more killings.

Norris Hall, about 9:30 A.M. The gunman entered Norris Hall, an engineering building. Then he chained the doors behind him. He climbed the stairs to the second floor. Inside Room 207, students in a German class were listening to Professor Christopher James Bishop. Suddenly, they began to hear unusual sounds outside the classroom. Some students thought the noises came from a construction site on campus. Others were not so sure. The noises sounded more like gunshots.

The door to the classroom swung open, and a young student walked inside. He wore a maroon cap and a dark vest. He aimed a pistol at Professor Bishop and shot him in the head. The students immediately tried to hide under the desks. But the gunman walked up and down the aisles, firing relentlessly. He emptied two or three shots into each student.

Trey Perkins was among the few who survived. The killer "never said a word the whole time," Perkins said. "I've never seen a straighter face. . . . There were a couple of screams, but for the most part it was eerily silent, other than the gunfire."[3] The gunman left Room 207. But those students who were still alive feared that he might return.

One of those students was twenty-year-old Derek O'Dell. The gunman had shot O'Dell's arm. O'Dell and others put their feet against the door to keep it closed if the killer returned.

Next door, in Room 211, Professor Jocelyne Couture-Nowak was teaching French. Couture-Nowak could hear what she thought were gunshots. "That's not what I

Derek O'Dell, a biology major at Virginia Tech, was shot in the arm during his German class in Norris Hall on April 16, 2007. With him is one of his dogs, Dallas.

think it is, is it?" she said to the class.[4] But students reassured her that it was noise from the construction site.

The gunman entered the classroom and killed Professor Couture-Nowak. Then he began killing students. "He just started down the rows of desks, shooting people multiple times," recalled student Colin Goddard. Goddard was shot in the leg and pretended to be dead. "Nobody tried to get up and be a hero," he added.[5]

Clay Violand recalled, "After every shot I thought, 'O.K., the next one is me.' Sometimes after a shot I would hear a quick moan, or a slow one or a grunt, or a quiet, reserved yell from one of the girls."[6]

The killer returned to Room 207. "I knew if he got back through that door we would all be dead," said O'Dell.[7] He and other students tried to keep it shut. The killer tried to push his way in. He fired through the door, injuring students inside.

8

The killer also returned to Room 211. "He came in and started going around the room again, shooting people," Colin Goddard said later.[8] Goddard was shot in the shoulder and again in the back. By the time the killer was finished, eleven students in Room 211 along with Professor Couture-Nowak were dead.

A similar scene was repeated in two other classrooms. In Room 206, the gunman killed Professor G. V. Loganathan and nine of his students. Next door was

Blacksburg police officers run near Norris Hall on April 16, 2007, the day of the massacre.

Room 204. Seventy-six-year-old Liviu Librescu was teaching an engineering class. When the gunman tried to enter, Professor Librescu blocked his way. This gave his students a few extra moments to head for the windows. Librescu was killed protecting his students; only one was shot dead.

Police arrived and got into the building. Upstairs, the killer, who would soon be identified as Seung-Hui Cho, put his pistol up to his head and killed himself.

Anatomy of a killing spree

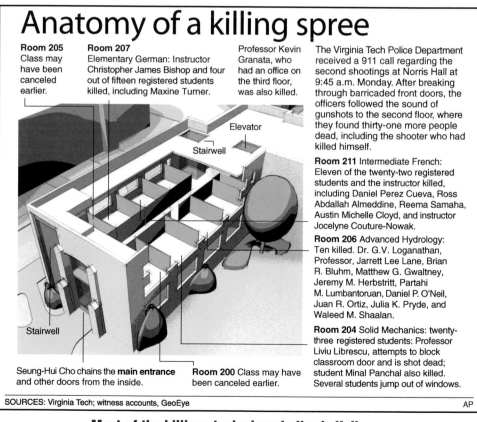

Room 205 Class may have been canceled earlier.

Room 207 Elementary German: Instructor Christopher James Bishop and four out of fifteen registered students killed, including Maxine Turner.

Professor Kevin Granata, who had an office on the third floor, was also killed.

Elevator

Stairwell

The Virginia Tech Police Department received a 911 call regarding the second shootings at Norris Hall at 9:45 a.m. Monday. After breaking through barricaded front doors, the officers followed the sound of gunshots to the second floor, where they found thirty-one more people dead, including the shooter who had killed himself.

Room 211 Intermediate French: Eleven of the twenty-two registered students and the instructor killed, including Daniel Perez Cueva, Ross Abdallah Almeddine, Reema Samaha, Austin Michelle Cloyd, and instructor Jocelyne Couture-Nowak.

Room 206 Advanced Hydrology: Ten killed. Dr. G.V. Loganathan, Professor, Jarrett Lee Lane, Brian R. Bluhm, Matthew G. Gwaltney, Jeremy M. Herbstritt, Partahi M. Lumbantoruan, Daniel P. O'Neil, Juan R. Ortiz, Julia K. Pryde, and Waleed M. Shaalan.

Room 204 Solid Mechanics: twenty-three registered students: Professor Liviu Librescu, attempts to block classroom door and is shot dead; student Minal Panchal also killed. Several students jump out of windows.

Stairwell

Seung-Hui Cho chains the **main entrance** and other doors from the inside.

Room 200 Class may have been canceled earlier.

SOURCES: Virginia Tech; witness accounts, GeoEye

AP

Most of the killings took place in Norris Hall.

CHAPTER 2

The Victims

NOT INCLUDING CHO'S SUICIDE, THE VIRGINIA TECH shootings claimed the lives of thirty-two people. Among them was Dr. Liviu Librescu, the engineering professor who died defending his students.

Librescu was a Jew, born in the Romanian city of Ploiesti in 1930. During World War II, Jews like Librescu faced extreme harassment, abuse, and violence from the German Nazis. They were rounding up Jews by the hundreds of thousands. Then the Jews were shipped off to death camps and murdered or to work camps where they were barely fed and forced to perform intense labor. This nightmare was known as the Holocaust. Librescu was among those who survived.

In 1978, Librescu and his family were permitted by the communist government to leave Romania for Israel. Then in 1985, Librescu moved to the United States to teach at Virginia Tech. As his son said, during the massacre

Above are professor Liviu Librescu and his wife, Marlena. Liviu Librescu saved the lives of several students by blocking the gunman, Seung-Hui Cho, during the shooting.

he was unafraid "to die in the place he loved the most, the classroom."[1]

Other Professors Killed

Several other teachers were also killed during the massacre. Jocelyne Couture-Nowak, a French instructor, had moved to Virginia Tech from Canada eight years earlier. Her husband, Jerzy Nowak, is also a professor there.

Kevin Granata was an engineering professor. He was also a well-known researcher in the field of cerebral palsy. This is an illness that affects muscles and joints. Granata wanted to give victims of cerebral palsy a better chance

12

to overcome their illness. Granata heard the shootings on April 16. Immediately, "he came out of his office to see what was going on and he was trying to help people," said his brother Paul Granata.[2]

Another teacher who was killed in the massacre was Christopher James Bishop. He taught German at Virginia Tech and ran an exchange program. Bishop selected outstanding students from his class to study at Darmstadt University of Technology in Germany. A spokesman from Darmstadt said, "Of course many persons knew him personally and are deeply, deeply shocked about his death."[3]

Professor G. V. Loganathan was also a victim of the shootings. Born in India, Loganathan was an engineering professor. He began teaching at Virginia Tech in 1981. He received the Outstanding Faculty Award and the Dean's Award for Excellence in Teaching from the college.

Students Who Were Murdered

Twenty-eight students including Cho also were shot dead. Freshman Henry Lee was born in China. Lee came to the United States with his parents when he was still a child. He worked hard to learn English. He eventually graduated high school as one of the top students in his class. His principal, Susan Willis, recalled his speech at graduation: "He said . . . 'Imagine sitting in class not knowing the

13

Full List of Those Killed by Cho

Students

Ross Abdallah Alameddine	Twenty-year-old sophomore English major
Brian Bluhm	Twenty-five-year-old graduate student of water resources
Ryan Clark	Twenty-two-year-old senior with triple major in psychology, biology, and English
Austin Cloyd	Eighteen-year-old freshman international-studies major
Daniel Perez Cueva	Twenty-one-year-old international-relations major
Mathew Gregory Gwaltney	Twenty-four-year-old graduate student in civil and environmental engineering
Caitlin Hammaren	Nineteen-year-old sophomore with double major in international studies and French
Jeremy Herbstritt	Twenty-seven-year-old graduate student in civil engineering
Rachael Elizabeth Hill	Eighteen-year-old freshman studying biology
Emily Jane Hilscher	Nineteen-year-old freshman animal-and-poultry-sciences major
Jarrett Lane	Twenty-two-year-old senior civil-engineering major
Matt La Porte	Sophomore political science and leadership major
Henry J. Lee	Freshman double major in computer engineering and French
Partahi Lumbantoruan	Thirty-one-year-old graduate student in civil engineering
Lauren McCain	Twenty-year-old freshman planning to major in international studies
Daniel O'Neil	Twenty-two-year-old graduate student in engineering
Juan Ortiz	Twenty-six-year-old graduate student in civil engineering

Full List of Those Killed by Cho

Students

Minal Panchal	Twenty-six-year-old graduate student in building sciences
Erin Peterson	Eighteen-year-old freshman planning to major in international relations
Michael Pohle	Twenty-three-year-old senior biological-sciences major
Julia Pryde	Twenty-three-year-old graduate student in biological-systems engineering
Mary Karen Read	Nineteen-year-old interdisciplinary-studies major
Reema Samaha	Eighteen-year-old freshman with an interest in dancing
Waleed Mohammed Shaalan	Thirty-two-year-old doctoral student in civil engineering
Leslie Sherman	Sophomore history and international-studies major
Maxine Turner	Senior chemical-engineering major
Nicole White	Twenty-year-old junior international-studies major

Faculty

Christopher James Bishop	Thirty-five-year-old German professor
Jocelyne Couture-Nowak	French professor
Kevin Granata	Forty-six-year-old biomechanics professor and researcher
Liviu Librescu	Seventy-six-year-old aeronautical-engineering professor and researcher
G. V. Loganathan	Fifty-one-year-old civil- and environmental-engineering professor

language. Now I am No. 2 in my class.' It was such a proud moment."[4]

Reema Samaha was a gifted actor who received an award for her performance in *Fiddler on the Roof.* A friend, Luann McNabb, recalled tearfully, "She was so full of joy."[5]

Ross Alameddine was known for his sharp wit. After the killings, students created a memorial to Alameddine on Facebook.com. His friend Zach Allen wrote, "You're such an amazing kid, Ross. You always made me smile."[6]

Matthew La Porte had attended a military school in Pennsylvania and received a scholarship to Virginia Tech. Dane Rogich grew up with La Porte. "From here, to military school, to college—it was amazing," Rogich recalled. "And then he was gone."[7]

Before attending Virginia Tech, Leslie Sherman played basketball at West Springfield High School in Virginia. "She was very spirited," said Deppika R. Chadive, a teammate. "She was always very enthusiastic. Even if we were down 50 points, she would always give us a pat on the back." Chadive added that Sherman hoped to become a historian. "We used to tell her 'It's illegal to love history as much as you do.'"[8]

Ryan Clark was a member of the school's marching band and one of the most popular students. "I remember vividly thinking," said David McKee, director of the band, "'This is an act! This can't be real.'" A close friend,

Messages and a photograph of Leslie Sherman grace one of the many memorial boards set up along on the campus of Virginia Tech on April 18, 2007, two days after the shooting.

Michael Pohle, center, is comforted by a priest after funeral services for his son, also named Michael Pohle.

Melissa Dowd, added: "He had the personality—open, nonjudgmental—that everyone works their entire life to have."[9]

Michael Pohle was a senior at Virginia Tech. The vice principal of his high school, Craig Blanton, recalled that he had "a bunch of job interviews and was all set to start his postcollegiate life. He was just a good person."[10]

Senior Jarret Lee Lane was remembered by his high school coach, Todd Lusk: "Not the type of athlete you'd picture. But he had the heart of a champion."[11] Lane was the captain of four different athletic teams in high school. He also earned a 4.0 average in his studies.

All of these lives were cut brutally short by the tragedy at Virginia Tech.

3

Portrait of a Killer

THE MURDERER RESPONSIBLE FOR THE TERRIBLE massacre was a senior at Virginia Tech. His name was Seung-Hui Cho. He was a lonely, isolated youth, with a history of emotional problems. Cho was extremely angry at the world around him and plotted a violent revenge.

Early Life of the Killer

Seung-Hui Cho was born in Seoul, South Korea. His family could only afford a small apartment. Finally, Cho's father, Seung-Tae Cho, went to the oil fields in Saudi Arabia. There he found a job and sent money home.

As a child, Seung-Hui Cho was different from other boys his age. He rarely spoke. As his great aunt Kim Yang-Soon recalled, "When I told his mother that he was a good boy, quiet but well behaved, she said she would rather have him respond to her when talked to."[1]

Eventually, Seung-Tae Cho returned from Saudi Arabia.

This undated photo of Seung-Hui Cho was released by the Virginia State Police after the shootings. The photo was taken during an unrelated matter months before the massacre.

He and his wife, Kim Hwang, decided to leave South Korea. They had relatives in the United States and hoped that its schools might help their son. They eventually settled in Centreville, Virginia, in the early 1990s. Centreville has a large South Korean community. Seung-Tae and Kim went to work at a local dry cleaners.[2]

Seung-Hui Cho went to a youth group at the family's local church. "Cho was a smart student who could understand the meaning of the Bible," said his minister. But he did not fit in with the other young people, who regularly bullied him.[3] Cho ran into similar problems in high school. He rarely spoke in class. But when he did say something, Cho's voice was low with a heavy accent. "As soon as he started reading," said a classmate, "the whole class started laughing and pointing and saying, 'Go back to China.'"[4]

As a result, Cho kept to himself and barely spoke to

anyone "like he had a broken heart," said his neighbor Abdul Shash.[5]

Life at Virginia Tech

In 2003, Cho began studies at Virginia Tech. Other students noticed that he was quiet. His roommates invited him to a fraternity party on the campus. But Cho rarely showed any expression on his face. So, they could not ever tell if he had enjoyed it. During the rest of his time at Virginia Tech, he mostly stayed by himself.

Andy Koch, suitemate of Seung-Hui Cho, would often return to his dorm to find Cho standing in the hall, staring out a window that offered a view of West Ambler Johnston Hall.

During his junior year, Cho attended a writing class taught by well-known poet Nikki Giovanni. Cho's poems contained images of death and other bizarre references. These bothered the other students. As a result, Giovanni told Cho that he must change the content of his poems or leave. "You can't make me," he said, defiantly.[6]

"You can't make me."

—Seung-Hui Cho, when asked by a professor to change the disturbing content of his poems

Eventually Lucinda Roy, one of the directors of the writing program, began tutoring Cho herself, instead of having him attend Giovanni's class. Professor Roy recalled that he hid his face behind sunglasses and a cap. "He seemed to be crying behind his sunglasses," she said.[7] Professor Roy suggested that Cho go to the counseling program on the Virginia Tech campus. Cho refused.

In 2005, Cho began stalking two young women at Virginia Tech. He called them on the telephone and went to their rooms. When one of the women called local police, the authorities warned Cho about his behavior. This upset Cho, and he told a roommate that he was considering suicide. As a result, the roommate reported this incident. Soon afterward, Cho was referred to a mental health clinic.

At the Carilion St. Albans Psychiatric Hospital, Cho

was examined by a doctor. A report stated that Cho's "affect [emotion] is flat and mood is depressed." But it added "his insight and judgment are normal."[8] The clinic released Cho but urged him to seek counseling.

In fall 2006, after becoming a senior, Cho attended another writing class. He wrote two plays that were extremely violent. "When we read Cho's plays, it was like something out of a nightmare," said a classmate, Ian MacFarlane. One of the plays was titled *Richard McBeef.* Cho's main character was a boy who was physically abused by his stepfather, Richard. The boy also believed that his father had been murdered by Richard. He says over and over again that he must kill his stepfather.[9]

Planning the Massacre

In February 2007, Cho purchased a handgun over the Internet. The gun was sent to a pawn shop, where Cho picked it up. A month later he bought an automatic pistol from a store.

In Virginia, an adult with proper identification can purchase a firearm. The store conducts a quick background check on the computer. This ensures that the customer does not have a criminal record or a history of mental illness. Apparently, Cho's visit to the mental health clinic did not show up on the background check.

Later in March, Cho shot targets at a local firing range.

This is an exterior view of the JND Pawnbrokers in Blacksburg, Virginia, where Seung-Hui Cho received one of the handguns used in the massacre.

In early April, Cho recorded a series of videotapes. On them, he filmed himself delivering an angry speech aimed at the students of Virginia Tech. "You had everything you wanted," he said. "Your Mercedes [car] wasn't enough, you brats? Your golden necklaces weren't enough, you snobs?"[10]

On Monday April 16, Cho arose early. One of his roommates, Joe Aust, saw him sitting in front of his computer. Another student, Karan Grewal, later saw him in the bathroom. By 7:00 A.M., Cho was on his way to West Ambler Johnston Hall. There he killed Emily Hilscher and Ryan Clark. Afterward, he returned to his room, then went to a nearby post office and mailed the videotapes to NBC News.

It was soon after that Cho walked to Norris Hall where he continued the terrible massacre.

CHAPTER

4

Why Did He Commit Mass Murder?

IN THE UNITED STATES, ONLY A SMALL NUMBER OF killings are mass murders. These are defined as those with five or more victims in a very short period. Generally, they are carefully planned by the killers. Most mass killers are males. Experts believe that several factors may influence an individual like Seung-Hui Cho to commit mass murder.

Biological Factors

The front of the brain acts as a brake on a person's emotions. When processing anger, the brain directs a person to stop and think before acting. But the brains of mass murderers are different. There is less activity in the front of the brain. This also means there is less sympathy for other people.

In 1998, after killing his parents at home, fifteen-year-old Kipland Kinkel killed two students and wounded twenty-three others in the cafeteria of Thurston High School in Springfield, Oregon. When Kinkel was examined, doctors found less activity than normal in the front part of his brain.

Kinkel had been treated for depression, much like Cho. The doctors treated Kinkel with medication. Kinkel was also angry at his parents. He believed that they had mistreated him. The day before the shooting, Kinkel had gotten into trouble for having a gun in school. His father had picked him up from the police department and had words with him.

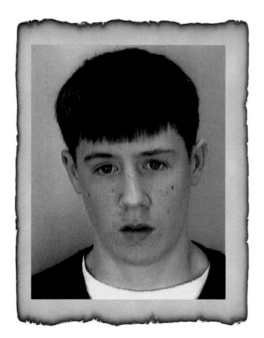

In his writings, Cho talked about a character who was abused by his father. But investigators do not know if similar abuse occurred to Cho.

Police took a photo of fifteen-year-old Kipland Kinkel on May 22, 1998, after he was arrested for the murder of his parents and students at Thurston High School.

Cho and Columbine

Investigators do know that Cho was a loner. Other students laughed at him in class and bullied him. In this way, he was similar to Eric Harris and Dylan Klebold. In fact, Cho praised "Eric and Dylan" in his writings.[1] On April 20, 1999, these two boys began shooting at students and faculty at Columbine High School in Littleton, Colorado. In the school library, they killed ten students and wounded twelve others. When the violence was over, they killed themselves. A total of fifteen people died, including the two killers.

Klebold and Harris considered themselves outsiders. Much like Cho, Klebold was quite shy. He also felt a great deal of anger toward his parents as well as other students. Klebold believed that they did not care about him. Harris shared these feelings. He even created a Web site where he talked about taking revenge on other people.

After Columbine, the government studied school violence. The study revealed that many killers suffered from severe depression, like Cho. According to Professor Diane Follingstad, "People will often say that the killer was such a quiet boy. Then you talk to the family and find out he's had three previous hospitalizations and was mumbling something he was angry about for weeks."[2]

Psychologists are also convinced that mass murderers do not simply snap, or act on the spur of the moment.

Eric Harris, left, and Dylan Klebold, walk their school's hallway in a video made by them months before their killing spree.

Generally, they plan the killings for weeks in advance. Cho bought and practiced with guns. He also made a series of videos. Harris and Klebold spent time gathering weapons and planning the killings. "Snapping is a misnomer," according to Dr. Michael Welner of New York University School of Medicine.[3]

Frequently, the killers believe that they have lost control of their lives. This sense of powerlessness builds and builds. Finally, they decide to regain control by striking back at the world. Then they usually blame their victims for the murders. Before the Virginia Tech massacre, Cho wrote, "I didn't have to do this. I could have fled. But no, I will no longer run. . . . You forced me into a corner and gave me only one option. The decision was yours. Now you have blood on your hands that will never wash off."[4]

Cho also sent videotapes to NBC News. In the tapes, he revealed that he was looking for recognition. He felt negatively toward himself. Cho also felt that other students paid no attention to him. A mass killing, Cho believed, would grab their attention. It would also make him an important person. "Thanks to you," he said in the videos, "I die like Jesus Christ." Cho had convinced himself that he was just as important as Christ.[5]

The killers "may think 'I may never amount to much,'" explained psychologist Jana Martin, "'but I'm going to die amounting to something. This is my final mark on the world, my final statement.'"[6]

Many factors led to Cho's massacre. But the killings would have been impossible without weapons.

Someone put up a yellow ribbon in memory of the Virginia Tech shooting victims outside the post office in Blacksburg, Virginia, from which Seung-Hui Cho sent a package to NBC News.

Gun Control

IN THE UNITED STATES THERE ARE ABOUT 260 MILLION guns. Approximately one quarter of these are handguns. Cho used two handguns at Virginia Tech. More Americans own guns than any other people in the world. Each day, twelve people under the age of nineteen die from gunfire in the United States.[1]

Gun-Control Law

In 1993, the U.S. Congress passed the Brady Handgun Violence Prevention Act. This bill was designed to make it harder for people to purchase guns. The Brady Law set up a criminal background-check system. This system checks to see if a person who wants to purchase a gun has committed a crime. Gun stores are required to run a background check on all customers before selling them a weapon.

The Brady Law prohibits a weapon from being sold to

Roanoke Firearms owner John Markell holds a Glock 9mm. The gun is similar to the one sold in his gun shop to Seung-Hui Cho about a month before the killings.

a criminal who has served a year in jail. In addition, anyone who has spent time in a mental institution cannot buy a gun.

Seung-Hui Cho had been required to receive psychological counseling. But he had not been in a mental institution. Therefore, his name did not show up on the database. Since he was over twenty-one, he could buy one weapon per month. Cho bought one handgun in February and another in March.

After the shootings at Virginia Tech, Virginia Governor Tim Kaine decided to tighten up the state law. Any people receiving mental-health counseling now have their names put in the database. They are prohibited from buying a gun. This might have prevented Cho from obtaining a weapon.

The Debate on Gun Control

Some Americans oppose tighter gun control laws. They point to the Second Amendment to the U.S. Constitution.

It states that "the people" have a right "to keep and bear arms." One group that strongly supports this right is the National Rifle Association (NRA). The NRA believes that gun-control laws violate the Constitution. Anyone who is not a criminal, according to the NRA, should have the right to own a weapon.

In fact, some people argue that more people, not fewer, should own guns. In 2006, a bill was introduced into the Virginia state legislature to allow students with gun permits to bring weapons to school. But the bill was defeated.

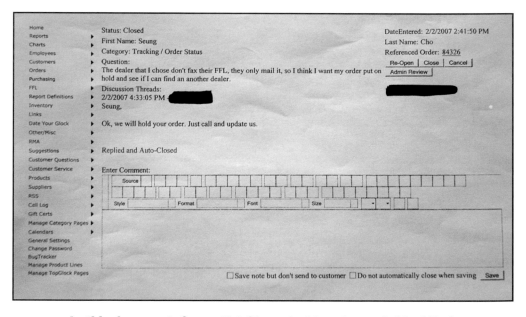

In this document, Seung-Hui Cho puts his order on hold while he searches for another gun dealer. A handgun picked up by Cho at a Virginia pawnbroker was bought from a Web site.

This was a mistake, according to Larry Pratt. He is executive director of Gun Owners of America. Students and teachers should have been permitted to carry guns, Pratt said. Then, Cho might have been stopped. "When will we learn that being defenseless is a bad defense?" Pratt stated.[2] Philip Van Cleave, president of the Virginia Citizens Defense League, agreed. Cho's massacre "was a major failure of gun control laws," he said. "Kids were unable to defend themselves."[3]

Six hundred thousand criminals were prevented from buying guns since 1994.

Supporters of this position point out that even with gun-control laws, potential killers get guns. At gun shows, merchants can sell guns without doing background checks. And young people under twenty-one often get an older friend to buy guns.

Nevertheless, supporters of gun control believe it works. Advocates of the Brady Law point out that six hundred thousand criminals were prevented from buying guns since 1994. They also think more guns on campus would just breed more violence. Tighter gun-control laws might have been enough to prevent Cho from committing mass murder. But it is impossible to be sure.

After the Disaster

AFTER LEARNING OF THE DISASTER AT VIRGINIA TECH, President George W. Bush spoke to the American people. Bush said that, "schools should be places of sanctuary and safety."[1]

The Days After

Following the massacre, Virginia Tech canceled classes for the rest of the week. On Tuesday, April 17, there was a large ceremony on campus. Students, faculty, and administrators gathered to remember the people who had been killed and wounded in the massacre.

President Bush traveled from Washington to the Virginia Tech campus to attend the gathering. "This is a day of mourning for Virginia Tech, and it is a day of sadness for our entire nation," the President said. "By the end of [yesterday] morning, it was the worst day of violence on a college campus in American history—and for many of you here today, it was the worst day of your lives."[2]

Thousands of Virginia Tech students stand during the memorial attended by President George W. Bush on April 17, 2007, a day after the shootings on the campus.

Poet Nikki Giovanni also addressed the gathering:

We are Virginia Tech. We are sad today, and we will be sad for quite a while. We are not moving on, we are embracing our mourning. We are Virginia Tech. We are strong enough to stand tall tearlessly, we are brave enough to bend to cry, and we are sad enough to know that we must laugh again. We are Virginia Tech. . . . We will prevail. We will prevail. We will prevail. We are Virginia Tech.[3]

The day after the massacre, there were reported threats at other colleges. Students were told to not

Virginia Tech professor Nikki Giovanni speaks in Peoria, Illinois. She honors the shooting victims by wearing a "Hokies" pin. Virginia Tech students are called Hokies.

go to any classes at the University of Oklahoma. At the University of Georgia, Police Chief Jimmy Williamson spoke to reporters. He said, "we have a full-fledged police force with 74 sworn officers. . . . But there's no way to prevent shootings by a crazed person with a gun."[4]

Nevertheless, some Virginia Tech parents asked why the college had not done more. After the first two shootings on April 16, parents wondered why classes had not been canceled. "I guess we're a little curious as to why it took so long," said Kim Tate.[5] Her daughter attends Virginia Tech. She was wondering why the college officials had not ordered everyone out of class and back to his or her room.

Tributes for those killed and wounded came from across the United States. On Tuesday, April 17, the Washington Nationals, a major-league baseball team, wore

Virginia Tech hats. On other campuses, students announced that Friday, April 20, was "Orange and Maroon Effect Day." Orange and maroon are the Virginia Tech colors, and the students called themselves the Hokies. Students planned to wear these colors and hold memorials for the victims. "We are all part of the Hokie Nation now," one student said. He added that we are "touched by their tragedy and one in their healing."[6]

Memorial Services

On Friday, April 20, victims of the massacre were remembered at memorial services. Many of the services were held in Virginia. But others occurred outside the United States. In Israel, family and friends tearfully remembered Liviu Librescu. In Nova Scotia, people gathered at a memorial for Jocelyne Couture-Nowak. "It's a hard day," said the Reverend Alexander W. Evans at a service for Professor Kevin P. Granata. "But we're here to give thanks for his life."[7]

There was a special service on the Virginia Tech campus. Thirty-two maroon and orange balloons floated into the sky. On each balloon was the name of one of the people killed in the massacre. Small memorials of flowers were placed on the grass on one part of campus. There was a memorial to Seung-Hui Cho, the killer, as well.

Meanwhile, Cho's family expressed their sorrow at

Virginia Tech student Amber Moore releases balloons on April 20, 2007, that represent Virginia Tech shooting victims. Each balloon has a victim's name written on it.

what he had done. "He has made the world weep," wrote his sister, Sun-Kyung Cho, in a family statement. "We feel hopeless, helpless and lost. This is someone that I grew up with and loved. Now I feel like I didn't know this person. Our family is so very sorry for my brother's unspeakable actions."[8]

The Wounded Students

Not only were thirty-two victims killed in the Virginia Tech disaster. Fifteen others were wounded. Colin Goddard was shot three times in Room 211. The doctors decided not to remove the bullets. They were afraid it might make the wounds much worse. "Your body forms a cocoon, so it will always be part of you," said his mother, Anne Lynam Goddard. "My biggest hope is that this is how my son will remember this. I hope he can form a cocoon around it and not let it be his defining moment."[9]

Justin Klein was in a wheelchair after being shot three times. But he went back to school after the massacre. "My place is here, with my friends," he wrote. But psychologists warned that students might have a difficult time returning to the campus. "For some people," said psychologist Mark Lerner, "being back on that campus will be a really good thing for them. For others, it may be more than can be expected, too much for them to handle."[10]

On Monday April 23, 2007, classes resumed at

Virginia Tech. Many students returned. But others stayed at home for the rest of the semester. Professor Joe Merola tried to conduct his class, but it was too much for him. "I lost it halfway through class," he said. "I burst into tears and had to turn it over to the [college] counselors."[11]

To mark the return to classes, students released one thousand orange and maroon balloons into the air. "Every day, you wake up and you don't know what you should do," said Andrea Falletti, a student. "Everyone's like,

Virginia Tech student Colin Goddard, who was injured in the shooting, walks back to his seat after speaking at the funeral of professor Jocelyne Couture-Nowak.

'Should we do something? Should we try to have fun?' You almost feel guilty smiling in Blacksburg."[12]

On the college campus, counselors wore purple armbands with the words "May I help." They expected that many students would need counseling to deal with the tragedy. Two of David Patton's friends died in the massacre. " . . . I don't know how it's going to feel," he said, "seeing the empty seats in the classroom, noticing the people who aren't here anymore."[13]

But as Larry Hincker, Virginia Tech associate vice president of university relations said, ". . . we have got to move forward. As you can imagine, we cannot let this horror define Virginia Tech. We're going to do whatever we can to get this place on its feet again."[14]

Virginia Tech held its graduation on May 11, 2007. A short time later, Virginia Governor Tim Kaine appointed an eight-member panel to investigate the shootings. In August, they delivered their report. The panel said that the university should have told students about the first two killings in West Ambler Johnston Hall. Classes should have been immediately canceled and the university closed so that there would have been far fewer students in Norris Hall, where Cho continued his rampage. "Warning students, faculty and staff might have made a difference," the report said. This sent an important message to any college that might face a violent incident in the future.[15]

Deadliest School Shootings
in the United States

Date	Description	Total Death Toll*
April 16, 2007	Seung-Hui Cho kills thirty-two people and injures fifteen at Virginia Tech in Blacksburg, Virginia, before killing himself.	33
August 1, 1966	Charles Whitman kills fourteen people and injures thirty-one at the University of Texas after murdering his wife and mother earlier in the day.	16
April 20, 1999	Eric Harris and Dylan Klebold kill thirteen people and themselves at Columbine High School in Littleton, Colorado.	15
March 21, 2005	Jeff Weise kills his grandfather and companion before going to his high school in Red Lake, Minnesota, and killing seven people and finally himself.	10
October 3, 2006	Thirty-two-year-old Carl Charles Roberts IV kills five girls and injures five at West Nickel Mines Amish School before killing himself.	6
November 1, 1991	Gang Lu, a graduate student at the University of Iowa, shoots five people dead before killing himself.	6
March 24, 1998	Mitchell Johnson and Andrew Golden kill five people and injure ten others at Westside Middle School in Jonesboro, Arkansas.	5
May 21, 1998	Kipland Kinkel kills two students and injures twenty-three at Thurston High School in Springfield, Oregon, after shooting his parents dead at home.	4
May 4, 1970	National Guard Troops kill four student protestors and injure nine at Kent State University in Ohio.	4
October 28, 2002	Gulf War veteran and student Robert Flores shoots three professors dead before killing himself.	4

*Total death toll includes any people killed immediately prior to the school shooting as well as any suicides by the killers.

Chapter Notes

Chapter 1. Murder on Campus

1. Evan Thomas, "Making of a Massacre," *Newsweek*, April 30, 2007, p. 29.

2. Ibid.

3. Raymond Hernandez, "Inside Room 207, Students Panic at Rampage and Then Hold Off Gunman's Return," *The New York Times*, April 18, 2007, p. A19.

4. Nancy Gibbs, "Darkness Falls," *Time*, April 30, 2007, p. 49.

5. Thomas, p. 30.

6. Gibbs, p. 49.

7. Thomas, p. 30.

8. Ibid., p. 31.

Chapter 2. The Victims

1. Haviv Rettig, "Israeli Professor Killed in US Attack," *Jerusalem Post*, April 17, 2007, <http://www.jpost.com/servlet/Satellite?cid=1176152816138&pagename=Jpost%2FJPArticle%2FshowFull> (August 9, 2007).

2. Brian Wallheimer, "Granata: Tried to Help During Shooting," *Lafayette Journal & Courier*, April 18, 2007, <http://www.indystar.com/apps/pbcs.dll/article?AID=/20070418/LOCAL/704180522/1196/LOCAL> (August 9, 2007).

3. "The Virginia Tech Victims," *Time*, April 17, 2007, <http://www.time.com/time/nation/article/0,8599,1611345,00.html> (August 9, 2007).

4. Pam Belluck, "Intersecting on a Fateful Day, Lives That Spanned the Country and the World," *The New York Times*, April 18, 2007, p. A19.

5. Ibid.

6. "Some Had Made Their Marks, and Many Others Were Just Beginning," *The New York Times*, April 18, 2007, p. A21.

7. Ibid.

8. Ibid.

9. Andrew Romano, "Lost Lives," *Newsweek*, April 30, 2007, p. 32.

10. Ibid.

11. Ibid., p. 35.

Chapter 3. Portrait of a Killer

1. N. R. Kleinfield, "Before Deadly Rage, a Lifetime Consumed by a Troubling Silence," *The New York Times*, April 22, 2007, p. 1.

2. Ibid., p. A26.

3. Evan Thomas, "Making of a Massacre," *Newsweek*, April 30, 2007, p. 24.

4. Ibid., p. 26.

5. Kleinfield, p. A26.

6. Thomas, p. 26.

7. Manny Fernandez and Marc Santora, "In Words and Silence, Hints of Anger and Isolation," *The New York Times*, April 18, 2007, p. A1.

8. Thomas, p. 28.

9. Fernandez and Santora, p. A1.

10. Thomas, p. 24.

Chapter 4. Why Did He Commit Mass Murder?

1. Evan Thomas, "Making of a Massacre," *Newsweek*, April 30, 2007, p. 24.

2. Jeffrey Kluger, "Inside a Mass Murderer's Mind," *Time*, April 19, 2007, <http://www.time.com/time/printout/0,8816,1612368,00.html> (May 1, 2007).

3. Ibid.

4. Sharon Pritz, "Updates on Cho," *Collegiate Times*, April 18, 2007, <http://www.collegiatetimes.com/416archive/Wednesday.html> (August 9, 2007).

5. Kluger.

6. Sharon Begley, "The Anatomy of Violence," *Newsweek*, April 30, 2007, <http://www.msnbc.com/id/18248728/site/newsweek/page/4/> (August 9, 2007).

Chapter 5. Gun Control

1. Ian Murray, "The U.S. Gun-Control Debate: A Critical Look," *Encyclopedia Britannica Online*, May 5, 2007, <http://www.britannica.com/eb/article-9344384/The-US-Gun-Control-Debate-A-Critical-Look> (May 9, 2007).

2. Warren Fiske, "Gun Control Laws Scrutinized in Wake of Virginia Tech Shootings," *The Virginian-Pilot Online*, April 30, 2007, <http://home.hamptonroads.com/stories/print.cfm?story=123742&ran=181840> (May 15, 2007).

3. Ibid.

Chapter 6. After the Disaster

1. David Harries, "President Bush Remarks on Tragedy," *CollegiateTimes*, April 16, 2007, <http://www.collegiatetimes.com/416archive/Monday.html> (August 9, 2007).

2. Shaila Dewan and John Broder, "Rampage Gunman Was Student; Warning Lag Tied to Bad Lead," *The New York Times*, April 18, 2007, p. A18.

3. "Transcript of Nikki Giovanni's Convocation Address," *Virginia Tech, Invent the Future*, http://www.vt.edu/remember/archive/giovanni_transcript.php> (July 17, 2007).

4. Tamar Lewin, "Unsettled Day on Campuses Around U.S.," *The New York Times*, April 18, 2007, p. A18.

5. Dewan and Broder, p. A18.

6. Cate Summers, "Maroon and Orange Effect Day," *CollegiateTimes*, April 18, 2007, <http://www.collegiatetimes.com/416archive/Wednesday.html> (August 9, 2007).

7. Ian Urbina and Manny Fernandez, "Memorial Services Held in U.S. and Around World," *The New York Times*, April 21, 2007, p. A13.

8. Ibid.

9. The Associated Press, "Va. Tech Wounded Face Deep Physical, Emotional Scars," *Virginia Tech Terror*, <http://www.virginiatechterror.com/index.php?option=com_content&task=view&id=53&Itemid=1> (August 9, 2007).

10. Ibid.

11. "Virginia Tech Students Return to Classes," April 24, 2007, <http://www.townhall.com/News/NewsArticle.aspx?contentGUID=2931b18f-33a0-4264-bc12-e9b4f7ae> (May 1, 2007).

12. Ibid.

13. "Balloons, Bells Honor the Virginia Tech Victims, *CNN.com*, April 24, 2007, <http://www.cnn.com/2007/US/04/23/va.tech/index.html> (August 9, 2007).

14. Joe Milicia and Michael Graczyk, The Associated Press, "Virginia Tech Now Tied to Kent, Texas," *The News & Observer*, April 29, 2007, <http://www.newsobserver.com/news/crime_safety/vatech/story/568826.html> (August 9, 2007).

15. Sophie Borland, "Virginia Tech Criticised over Massacre Response," *Telegraph*, August 31, 2007, <http://www.telegraph.co.uk/news/main.jhtml?xml=/news/2007/08/30/wtech130.xml> (October 22, 2007).

Glossary

automatic pistol—A gun that fires by pulling the trigger without reloading for each shot.

cerebral palsy—A paralysis from a brain injury that affects muscles and joints.

counseling—Receiving help with a psychological problem from a trained professional.

depression—A mental disorder that leaves an individual feeling constantly sad, often without any particular reason.

massacre—The killing of many people.

mass murder—The killing of five or more people in a short period.

memorial service—A ceremony to remember someone who has died.

Nazis—Members of a brutal German political party led by Adolf Hitler.

pawn shop—A store that gives or loans money to individuals in return for their possessions.

psychologist—A medical specialist trained in understanding human behavior.

resident advisor—Faculty member or student who lives in dorms to advise students.

sanctuary—A safe place.

stalking—Relentlessly following another person in a threatening way.

suicide—Taking one's own life.

Further Reading

Books

Brown, Brooks and Rob Merritt. *No Easy Answers: The Truth Behind Death at Columbine*. New York: Lantern Books, 2002.

Cothran, Helen. *Gun Control: Opposing Viewpoints*. San Diego: Greenhaven Press, 2002.

Egendorf, Laura K., ed. *Violence: Opposing Viewpoints*. San Diego, Calif.: Greenhaven Press, 2001.

Gold, Susan Dudley. *Gun Control*. New York: Benchmark Books, 2004.

Grapes, Bryan J., ed. *School Violence*. San Diego, Calif.: Greenhaven Press, 2000.

Orr, Tamra. *Violence in Our Schools: Halls of Hope, Halls of Fear*. New York: Franklin Watts, 2003.

Scott, Darrell and Beth Nimmo with Steve Rabey. *Rachel's Tears: The Spiritual Journey of Columbine Martyr Rachel Scott*. Nashville, Tenn.: Thomas Nelson Publishers, 2000.

Internet Addresses

CNN.com—Special Reports: Massacre at Virginia Tech
<http://www.cnn.com/specials/2007/virginiatech.shootings/>

Virginia Tech Massacre.com
<http://www.virginiatechmassacre.com>

Virginia Tech—We Remember
<http://www.vt.edu/remember>

Index

B
Bishop, Christopher James, 7, 13
Brady Handgun Violence
    Prevention Act, 30–31, 33
Bush, George W., 34

C
Carilion St. Albans Psychiatric
    Hospital, 22–23
Cho, Seung-Hui, 10, 11, 13, 26,
    30, 31, 33, 37, 39
    and the Columbine High
        School massacre, 27–29
    life at Virgina Tech, 19–25
Cho, Seung-Tae, 19–20
Citizens Defense League, 33
Clark, Ryan, 5, 6, 16, 18, 24
Columbine High School
    massacre, 27–29
Couture-Nowak, Jocelyne, 7–8,
    9, 12

G
Giovanni, Nikki, 22, 35
Goddard, Colin, 8, 9, 39
Granata, Kevin, 12–13, 37
gun control, 30–33

H
Harris, Eric, 27–28
Haugh, Heather, 5, 6
Hilscher, Emily, 5, 6, 24

K
Kaine, Tim, 31
Kinkel, Kipland, 26
Klebold, Dylan, 27–28
Klein, Justin, 39

L
La Porte, Matthew, 16
Lane, Jarret, Lee, 18
Librescu, Liviu, 10, 11–12, 37
Loganathan, G. V., 9, 13

N
National Rifle Association (NRA),
    32
NBC News, 24, 29
Norris Hall, 6–10, 24

O
O'Dell, Derek, 7, 8
"Orange and Maroon Effect
    Day," 37

P
Perkins, Trey, 7
Pohle, Michael, 18

R
Roy, Lucinda, 22

S
Samaha, Reema, 16
Sherman, Leslie, 16
Steger, Charles, 6, 41

T
Tate, Kim, 36
Thornhill, Karl, 5, 6

V
Violand, Clay, 8

W
Washington Nationals, 36–37
West Ambler Johnston Hall, 5,
    24, 41
Willis, Susan, 13, 16

DATE